YOU'RE ROARSOME

An Hachette UK Company
www.hachette.co.uk

Summersdale Publishers Ltd
Part of Octopus Publishing Group Limited
Carmelite House
50 Victoria Embankment
LONDON
EC4Y 0DZ
UK

www.summersdale.com

Printed and bound in Malta

ISBN: 978-1-78685-812-2

Substantial discounts on bulk quantities of Summersdale books are available to corporations, professional associations and other organisations. For details contact general enquiries: telephone: +44 (0) 1243 771107 or email: enquiries@summersdale.com.

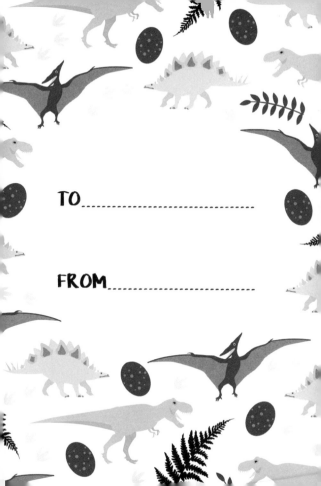

TO_____

FROM_____

You're perfect when you're comfortable being yourself.

ANSEL ELGORT

NOTHING CAN
DIM THE LIGHT
WHICH SHINES
FROM WITHIN.

MAYA ANGELOU

Believe you can and you're halfway there.

THEODORE ROOSEVELT

Be yourself—
EVERYONE ELSE IS
ALREADY TAKEN.

OSCAR WILDE

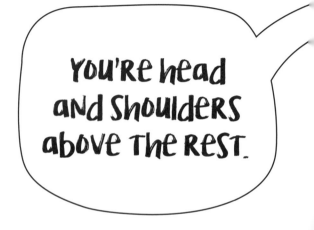

BE YOURSELF. THE WORLD WORSHIPS THE ORIGINAL.

INGRID BERGMAN

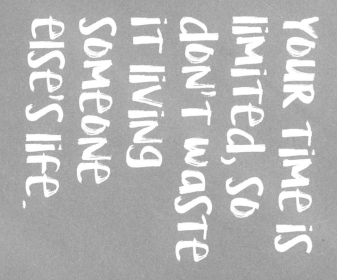

YOUR TIME IS
limited, so
don't waste
it living
someone
else's life.

STEVE JOBS

Think big and don't listen to people who tell you it can't be done. Life's too short to think small.

TIM FERRISS

**Ride the energy
of your own unique spirit.**

GABRIELLE ROTH

THE MORE YOU PRAISE AND CELEBRATE YOUR LIFE, THE MORE THERE IS IN LIFE TO CELEBRATE.

OPRAH WINFREY

As soon as you trust
yourself, you will
know how to live.

**JOHANN WOLFGANG
VON GOETHE**

BE IN LOVE
WITH YOUR LIFE,
EVERY DETAIL
OF IT.

JACK KEROUAC

ORIGINALITY IMPLIES
BEING BOLD ENOUGH
TO GO BEYOND
ACCEPTED NORMS.

ANTHONY STORR

LET US lEARN TO
SHOW OUR FRIENDSHIP
FOR a MAN WHEN
HE IS alive aND NOT
aFTER HE IS dead.

F. SCOTT FITZGERALD

YOU'RE ONLY HERE
FOR A SHORT VISIT.
DON'T HURRY, DON'T
WORRY. AND BE SURE
TO SMELL THE FLOWERS
ALONG THE WAY.

WALTER HAGEN

I DON'T WANT OTHER
PEOPLE TO DECIDE WHO I
AM. I WANT TO DECIDE
THAT FOR MYSELF.

EMMA WATSON

Expect problems and eat them for breakfast.

ALFRED A. MONTAPERT

**Just be yourself.
There is no one better.**

TAYLOR SWIFT

FIND ECSTASY
IN LIFE; THE MERE
SENSE OF LIVING
IS JOY ENOUGH.

EMILY DICKINSON

A good head and a
good heart are always a
formidable combination.

NELSON MANDELA

WHEREVER YOU GO,
go with all your heart.

CONFUCIUS

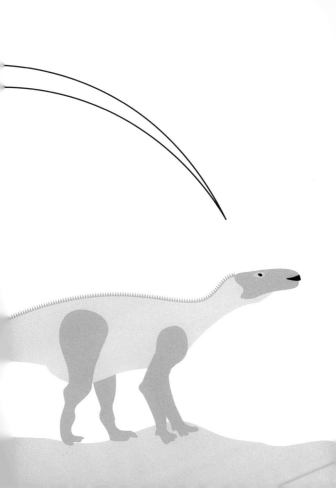

YOUR SUCCESS WILL BE DETERMINED BY YOUR OWN CONFIDENCE.

MICHELLE OBAMA

TRUST
YOURSELF.
YOU KNOW
MORE THAN
YOU THINK
YOU DO.

BENJAMIN SPOCK

We have to dare
to be ourselves,
however frightening
or strange that self
might prove to be.

MAY SARTON

**Talk to yourself
like you would to
someone you love.**

BRENÉ BROWN

IF YOU'RE PRESENTING YOURSELF WITH CONFIDENCE, YOU CAN PULL OFF PRETTY MUCH ANYTHING.

KATY PERRY

Be happy. It's one
way of being wise.

COLETTE

IF YOU THINK
YOU CAN DO IT,
YOU CAN.

JOHN BURROUGHS

**TO SUCCEED IN LIFE, YOU
NEED THREE THINGS: A
WISHBONE, A BACKBONE
AND A FUNNY BONE.**

REBA McENTIRE

FiND OUT who you aRE
and bE THAT PERSON...
FiND THAT TRUTH,
live THAT TRUTH
and EVERYTHING
ElSE will comE.

ELLEN DeGENERES

Rise above the
storm and you will
find the sunshine.

MARIO FERNÁNDEZ

I've got a theory that if you give 100 per cent all of the time, somehow things will work out in the end.

LARRY BIRD

MIGHTY OAKS
FROM LITTLE
ACORNS GROW.

PROVERB

The dreamers are the saviours of the world.

JAMES ALLEN

TELL ME, WHAT IS IT
YOU PLAN TO DO WITH
YOUR ONE wild AND
PRECIOUS LIFE?

MARY OLIVER

WHY FIT IN WHEN
YOU WERE BORN
TO STAND OUT?

DR SEUSS

STAY STRONG and be YOURSELf! IT'S The best Thing you can be.

CARA DELEVINGNE

YOU NEED TO BELIEVE
THAT YOU ARE GOOD
ENOUGH AND THAT
YOU CAN ACCOMPLISH
WHAT YOU SET YOUR
MIND TO DO.

DWAYNE 'THE ROCK' JOHNSON

Big shots are only
little shots who
keep shooting.

CHRISTOPHER MORLEY

IF IT'S IMPORTANT, YOU HAVE TO DO IT YOURSELF.

NEIL GAIMAN

**Those who bring sunshine
into the lives of others cannot
keep it from themselves.**

J. M. BARRIE

BE FAITHFUL
TO THAT WHICH
EXISTS NOWHERE
BUT IN YOURSELF.

ANDRÉ GIDE

WE ARE ALL DIFFERENT. DON'T JUDGE, UNDERSTAND INSTEAD.

ROY T. BENNETT

We were scared,
but our fear was
not as strong as
our courage.

MALALA YOUSAFZAI

**YOU CANNOT CHANGE
WHAT YOU ARE, ONLY
WHAT YOU DO.**

PHILIP PULLMAN

those who mind don't matter, and those who matter don't mind.

BERNARD BARUCH

It's **OK** to be powerful
in every way: to be big,
to take up space.

CLAIRE DANES

Follow your own star.

DANTE ALIGHIERI

IT IS NOT THE
MOUNTAIN WE
CONQUER BUT
OURSELVES.

EDMUND HILLARY

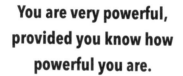

You are very powerful,
provided you know how
powerful you are.

YOGI BHAJAN

DIFFERENT IS **good**.
SO, DON'T FIT IN, DON'T
SIT STILL, **don't**
EVER TRY TO **be less**
THAN WHAT YOU ARE.

ANGELINA JOLIE

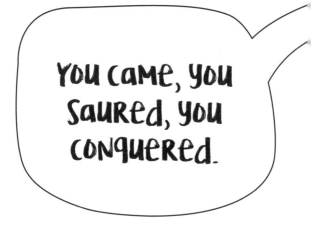

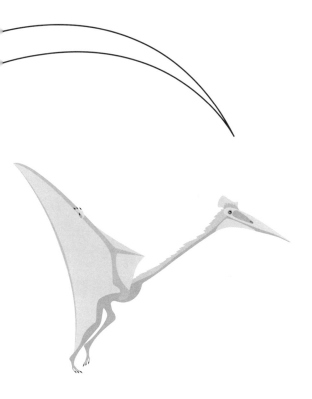

WE MUST
OVERCOME THE
NOTION THAT WE
MUST BE REGULAR...
IT ROBS YOU OF
THE CHANCE TO BE
EXTRAORDINARY.

UTA HAGEN

I NEVER lose sight of the fact that just being is fun.

KATHARINE HEPBURN

The formula of happiness and success is just being actually yourself, in the most vivid possible way you can.

MERYL STREEP

Never regret something that once made you smile.

AMBER DECKERS

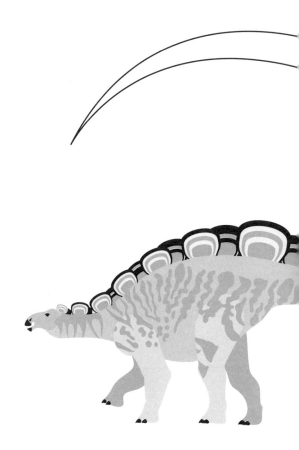

YOU ARE GOOD, YOU ARE GREAT, YOU ARE AMAZING.

AUSTIN CARLILE

**The reward for conformity
is that everyone likes
you except yourself.**

RITA MAE BROWN

THERE ARE SO
MANY GREAT THINGS
IN LIFE; WHY DWELL
ON NEGATIVITY?

ZENDAYA

ONCE YOU CHOOSE
HOPE, ANYTHING
IS POSSIBLE.

CHRISTOPHER REEVE

Live boldly.
Push yourself.
Don't settle.

JOJO MOYES

**ADVENTURE IS
WORTHWHILE
IN ITSELF.**

AMELIA EARHART

YOU DON'T NEED TO LOOK
like everybody else.
Love who you are.

LEA MICHELE

Accept the challenges so that you can feel the exhilaration of victory.

GEORGE S. PATTON

**Doubt whom you will,
but never yourself.**

CHRISTIAN NESTELL BOVEE

THE FINAL FORMING
OF A PERSON'S
CHARACTER LIES IN
THEIR OWN HANDS.

ANNE FRANK

Nurture your mind with great thoughts. To believe in the heroic makes heroes.

BENJAMIN DISRAELI

OPTIMISM IS THE
faith THAT LEADS
TO achievement.

HELEN KELLER

YOU HAVE
TO BELIEVE
IN YOURSELF.

SUN TZU

EVEN if
YOU FALL ON
YOUR FACE,
YOU'RE STILL
MOVING
FORWARD.

VICTOR KIAM

Beauty is perfect in its imperfections, so you just have to go with the imperfections.

DIANE VON FÜRSTENBERG

THE TRUE NOBILITY IS IN BEING SUPERIOR TO YOUR PREVIOUS SELF.

W. L. SHELDON

**Self-trust is the first
secret of success.**

RALPH WALDO EMERSON

UNFOLD YOUR
OWN MYTH.

RUMI

ACCEPT WHO YOU ARE; AND REVEL IN IT.

MITCH ALBOM

Life isn't about
finding yourself.
Life is about
creating yourself.

ANONYMOUS

BELIEVE IN YOUR FLYNESS; CONQUER YOUR SHYNESS.

KANYE WEST

Be yourself.
No one can ever
tell you you're
doing it wrong.

JAMES LEO HERLIHY

**Keep smiling, because life is
a beautiful thing and there's
so much to smile about.**

MARILYN MONROE

THINK BIG THOUGHTS
BUT RELISH SMALL
PLEASURES.

H. JACKSON BROWN JR

**A day without laughter
is a day wasted.**

NICOLAS CHAMFORT

FORTUNE

favours

THE BOLD.

LATIN PROVERB

ALWAYS BE YOURSELF... DO NOT GO OUT AND LOOK FOR A SUCCESSFUL PERSONALITY AND TRY TO DUPLICATE IT.

BRUCE LEE

IT WILL
NEVER BE
PERFECT, BUT
PERFECT IS
OVERRATED.
PERFECT IS
BORING.

TINA FEY ON LIFE

ONCE we believe in ourselves, we can risk curiosity, wonder, spontaneous delight, or any experience that reveals the human spirit.

E. E. CUMMINGS

Our greatest glory is not in never falling, but in rising every time we fall.

OLIVER GOLDSMITH

I'D RATHER AIM HIGH AND MISS, THAN AIM LOW AND HIT.

LES BROWN

Do a little more each day than you think you possibly can.

LOWELL THOMAS

IF YOU DON'T
LIVE YOUR LIFE THEN
WHO WILL?

RIHANNA

WHATEVER
YOU CAN DO OR
DREAM YOU CAN,
BEGIN IT; BOLDNESS
HAS GENIUS, POWER
AND MAGIC IN IT.

JOHN ANSTER

When you have confidence, you can have a lot of fun.

JOE NAMATH

**WHATEVER IS GOING
TO HAPPEN WILL
HAPPEN, WHETHER
WE WORRY OR NOT.**

ANA MONNAR

You wouldn't worry
so much about what
people may think of you
if you could know how
seldom they do.

OLIN MILLER

There's power in looking silly and not caring that you do.

AMY POEHLER

**Man cannot discover new
oceans unless he has the
courage to lose sight
of the shore.**

ANDRÉ GIDE

DREAMING, AFTER
ALL, IS A FORM
OF PLANNING.

GLORIA STEINEM

It is not wrong to be different. Sometimes it is hard, but it is not wrong.

ELIZABETH MOON

I DON'T
THINK
limits.

USAIN BOLT

EMBRACE
WHO YOU ARE.
LITERALLY. HUG
YOURSELF. ACCEPT
WHO YOU ARE.

ELLEN De**GENERES**

FOLLOW
YOUR INNER
MOONLIGHT;
DON'T
hide THE
MADNESS.

ALLEN GINSBERG

NEVER bend YOUR head. Always hold it high. LOOK THE WORLD STRAIGHT IN THE eye.

HELEN KELLER

This above all: to thine own self be true.

WILLIAM SHAKESPEARE

If you're interested in finding out more about our books, find us on Facebook at **Summersdale Publishers** and follow us on Twitter at **@Summersdale**.

www.summersdale.com

IMAGE CREDITS